The Young Athlete's Perspective

The Young Athlete's Perspective

TALENT DEVELOPMENT STORIES:
What They Want and Need

Graham Turner, PhD

The Young Athlete's Perspective

Copyright © 2023 Graham Turner, PhD

The moral rights of the author have been asserted. All rights reserved. No part of this publication may be reproduced, stored in or introduced into a retrieval system or transmitted in any form or by any means (electronic, mechanical, photocopying, recording or otherwise) without the prior written permission of the copyright owner of this book.

9 8 7 6 5 4 3 2 1

First Edition

ISBN 978-0-646-87571-2 (print)
ISBN 978-0-646-87572-9 (e-book)

Edited by John Coomer
Book cover and interior design by Jonathan Sainsbury
Author photograph by Jesse Spezza

TESTIMONIALS

'The stories in this book should open the eyes of parents, coaches and administration staff. Graham has gone into great depth to reveal how the athlete feels and how words can either be supportive or destructive. We don't know what it's like to be a young athlete in this climate, but we can listen, support, and help, when and where they need it. Well done Graham on going behind the scenes and listening to the voices of the young people of today. A great read that I've taken a lot of information from.'

—**Janelle Pallister Olympian,** High Performance Coach, Swimming Australia. Mother of World Champion Swimmer Lani Pallister.

'Helping young people achieve their potential is one of the most rewarding things you can do as a coach and this book contains many great ideas and thoughts on how to navigate the challenges of developing talent through an athlete's teenage years. It is a must read for anyone coaching and developing talent in all sports.'

—**Stuart Lancaster,** Senior Coach Leinster Rugby, former England Rugby Head Coach.

'As a former Australian netballer, pathway coach and parent of 3 young adults this book highlights many valuable learnings about supporting your child to navigate the bumpy "sport journey". A great read enjoy!'

>—**Jenny Borlase,** High Performance Netball Coach, 3 time Netball World Champion for Australia. Mother of Isobel, Australian Basketballer, James, Australian Football League player and Ella, junior champion Surf Life Saver.

'At last we have a book that includes the young athlete's perspective while simultaneously providing the reader tangible take-away's that have the potential to positively influence youth athlete development. I would highly recommend this book to anyone working in the youth athlete space.'

>—**Duncan Simpson PhD,** Director of Personal Development at IMG Academy, Florida USA.

'The coaching of athletes in any sport is tricky, let alone the added complexities that come with being within a talent pathway. This book is an absolute must for anyone that wants to improve their coaching and help young people maximise their potential.'

>—**Nick Levitt,** Head of Coaching at Brighton and Hove Albion, English Premier League. Former Head of Coaching at UK Coaching.

'Few resources focus on the experiences of the athletes themselves. Graham's book, based on both his extensive academic and practical experience, is a breakthrough in this area, providing an effective guide for all involved in developing athletes towards their potential.'

—**Craig Pickering PhD,** Olympian, Director of Performance Sustainability, Athletics Australia.

'An insightful set of narratives which clearly illustrate some of the contemporary issues surrounding coaching young people in sport. Graham has recounted and analysed these lived experiences from a holistic perspective, to provide thought provoking support for those guiding and influencing talent development.'

—**Lisa Gannon PhD,** Associate Professor. Welsh Gymnastics, Olympics Gymnastics commentator, former GB gymnast.

'An easy read with absolute golden nuggets in each story for coaches to understand their athletes better. A must-read for coaches or anyone seeking to develop the total athlete.'

—**Leanne Choo Olympian,** National Head Coach, Badminton Australia.

FOREWORD

If you are supporting and developing a talented athlete, then you care about their experience and want to do your best to help them improve and progress. You know that the odds are heavily stacked against them, but this won't stop you from encouraging their journey and supporting their dream.

This book features six stories told by young athletes about their talent development experiences in sport. It enables them to describe their unique view of what their talent development experience in sport is like for them. Each young athlete tells a personal story. They describe their own individual set of circumstances and provide a personal perspective that has been shaped by living in contemporary times.

These unique stories are shared in the hope that they may support coaches and parents to better connect with the young athlete's perspective. When considered together, these individual insights confirm the essence of the talent development experience and they reveal what every parent and coach supporting and developing the young athlete needs to know!

This book will provide you with valuable insights into key topics and issues, such as:

- ◆ How to support young athletes to progress in the sport that is right for them.
- ◆ How a positive talent development experience relies upon personalised and holistic athlete development.
- ◆ How to guide the young athlete through competing physical demands and psychological challenges.
- ◆ Why optimal athlete and coach collaboration relies upon a genuine relationship and authentic communication.
- ◆ How autonomy, connectedness and a sense of competence are critical to a young athlete's motivation.
- ◆ How to teach the young athlete to become the best learner.

The young athlete stories in this book are designed to stand alone and speak for themselves. They provide the young athlete's perspective on what they need and what they want in their own words. I invite you to listen.

CONTENTS

Testimonials	v
Foreword	ix
Introduction	1

Chapter 1

Sport Specialisation	5
George's Story – A Split Decision	5
Coming to the Crunch	8
The National Schools Championships	10
Back to Rugby	11
Time to Choose	12
Sport Specialisation – Key Takeaways	14
Talent Development Tips	16

Chapter 2

Identity	17
Eboni's Story – Two Worlds Collide	17
Countdown	18
'Netball First'	19
Nationals Weekend	20
Fair Play	21
Senior Netball	22
Planning Ahead	23

Identity – Key Takeaways	24
Talent Development Tips	26

Chapter 3

Growth, Maturation, Health and Wellbeing	27
Dan's Story	
– Standing Still but Moving Forwards	27
Treatment Plan	29
Small Steps	30
Moving On	31
Growth, Maturation, Health and Wellbeing	
– Key Takeaways	32
Talent Development Tips	35

Chapter 4

Self-Presentation	37
Rowan's Story – You've Got to Believe	37
Early Learning	38
Believing in Yourself!	39
Making Progress	41
Would You Believe It?	42
Self-Presentation – Key Takeaways	44
Talent Development Tips	46

Chapter 5

Self-Determination	47
Laura's Story – Finding a Way	47
A Difficult Life	48
Crisis of Confidence	49
Competition Day	52
A New Way Forward	53
Self-Determination – Key Takeaways	54
Talent Development Tips	56

Chapter 6
- Self-Regulation — 57
- Josh's Story – Fishing in the Dark — 57
  - Waiting — 58
  - The Final Trial — 60
  - The Big Shock — 62
- Self-Regulation – Key Takeaways — 64
- Talent Development Tips — 66

Conclusion — 67

Acknowledgements — 69

About the Author — 71

INTRODUCTION

My son was 13 and had been signed to a professional football (soccer) club since he was eight. At the end of the previous season, his coach told him that he had 'done ok', but needed to keep improving and stay fit over summer. Now the new season was only six weeks away, but 'lucky' for him I had worked in professional football for ten years, had a Masters Degree in Sport and Exercise Science and knew exactly how to get him fit:

> *'That's one done mate, well done. Stick to that pace, make sure you alternate legs when you turn,..........don't bend over now, stand up straight, regulate your breathing, in through your nose out through your mouth, ...you are going again in eighty seconds, ...one down seven to go.'*

His breathing was jagged, rasping and intrusive. He couldn't speak, all he could do was breathe. He wasn't in charge of his breathing – it was in charge of him. All he could do was fight to keep up with it. Sixty seconds passed.

'I'm not doing eight.'

'Twenty seconds to go, don't worry mate you'll be fine, take long slow breaths, get your mind right, are you ready? 10 seconds……………………… five, four, three, two, one, go!'

And he went again, and again, and again, and again, and again, and again, and again, and then he collapsed on the ground, his ribs writhing as he fought for air.

'That's brilliant mate, well done!'

He couldn't hear me. The only thing that mattered to him was air. Eventually he got up. As he walked past me to the car, he said:

'I'm never doing that again.'

Interval training finished, I started to drive. It was time for the car conversation. The car conversation is a time the child with 'talent' knows well. This is when the adult imparts their knowledge and the young person is required to listen.

However, this car conversation was different. I analysed his performance and I gave him feedback. He let me speak, and once I had finished giving my best advice, he said to me:

'Dad, you just don't understand the mentality of a thirteen- year -old.'

This time, instead of responding, I thought about what he had just said to me. It was the best thing I ever did.

On that day, we had shared the same time and space, but we had not lived the same experience. He was the only person who knew what it felt like to be him, and what mattered most was how he felt now. As for the future, that was his to determine. His words resonated and one question became crystalised in my mind.

> *'What is the best way to really help and support a young person involved in a sports talent development program?'*

Talent development was something I had studied, something I worked in and something I thought I knew, but my son was right. I didn't know what it was like for him. I didn't know what it was like to be a contemporary young athlete!

I needed to find an authentic way to relate to this experience, so I embarked upon a PhD designed to investigate the essence of the young person's experience in a sports talent development program. I was committed to finding a better way to help, so I sought out talented young athletes (male and female) from a range of different talent development programs in sport. I asked them how I could find out what their experience was really like. Their advice was clear and simple:

> *'Come and see what we do and ask us about it!'*

The six stories in this book come from my PhD study of young athletes' experiences of talent development in sport. My process relied upon building long-term relationships with these athletes that were characterised by friendship and trust. Each individual had a unique story to tell in their own words and they all demonstrated how their experience of talent development extended far beyond their time spent in training and competition. It came to influence every area of their lives.

Each young athlete confirmed that they learned to live with the expectation of continually striving to improve their performance. For as long as they could commit to this demand, they were prepared to search for ways to positively influence their progress. Each has willingly shared their story because they believe that the best way a parent or coach can help support this talent development process is to gain insight into what the experience is really like for them.

CHAPTER 1

SPORT SPECIALISATION

In this chapter, you will gain insights into how to:

- ◆ Support young athletes to progress in the sport that is right for them.
- ◆ Treat talent development as a shared relationship between coach, athlete and parents.
- ◆ Respect that each talented athlete is a unique individual.

GEORGE'S STORY
A SPLIT DECISION

George is 17. He plays rugby union and throws the discus. When he was an Under 16, he was picked to represent his country in both rugby and athletics.

George has been doing two sports for quite a while.

He started out playing rugby aged six and took up discus a few years later when he was about 12. He has done really well in both and by the age of 16 he was ranked number one in discus for his national age group and had also become a member of a professional Rugby Academy. The question that George was always asked was, 'Which one are you going to choose?' but at that time, he thought he had *another couple of more years at juggling* and was yet to make up his mind.

> *'I think I could probably be quite good at both, so I think something is going to happen that makes me choose one of them, but at the moment I don't really know.'*

George didn't need to choose because things were going well, very well in fact! When he was picked to play in his first representative rugby game, he was:

> *'Bouncing off the walls! Buzzing!'*

And when he put on that national shirt, it was the:

> *'Best moment of my life so far.'*

That game went well, and George was invited to the National Rugby Training Camp.

> *'An amazing weekend spent with some amazing people.'*

It culminated in selection for his country to play against France.

> *'Unbelievable experience playing for my country, one I'll always remember and hopefully not the last.'*

George was proud of his achievements in rugby. He had worked hard to earn them, especially as it was his first year of doing winter training for discus at the same time.

Previously, George had done a summer of athletics followed by a winter of rugby, and then tried to get back into athletics as fast as he could. He'd done that for the past three years but it hadn't worked very well. Last season in his opening competition, his first two attempts were no throws and then he threw 33 metres on his third (a standing throw). Over the season he increased his distance to 54 metres, but that wasn't the way it was supposed to happen. This year he wanted to start high and gradually increase.

> 'It's such a technical sport you can't take six months out and try and come back, your technique completely goes out of the window. So with me having quite a big year this year I wanted to kind of do a winter's training so, training nights are normally for me Tuesday night, Thursday night and then weekends are both Saturdays and Sundays whenever I am not playing rugby.'

As the rugby season came to an end, George had his Academy end-of-season review. His club told him that they were pleased with his progress and that:

> 'They understood that this year was gonna be quite a big year for me with athletics so they just said if you've got anything big coming up, just let us know and we'll let you have a lighter week of training.'

Now it was getting close to athletics season and

George was getting excited.

> 'Now rugby's finished, I can pretty much focus 100% on discus until rugby starts again.'

The National Schools Championships were in his sights. He had been three times before but the competition always came early in the season and he never felt like he had done his best. Last year he came third.

> 'From the National Schools, if you come first or second, you have the Schools Internationals, where you compete for your country!'

This would be the last chance he had to make it.

COMING TO THE CRUNCH

Winter training had brought dividends. George was throwing further and throwing well, but now training was more intense and becoming harder to cope with. And then came the injury.

> 'It was just one competition, but after a couple of throws I just had a really bad pain in my groin.'

George had never felt anything like it before and he wasn't sure what to expect next, but the following day it felt like it was completely better. That was good because George needed it to be right, he had rugby pre-season fitness testing coming up!

> 'So I went into testing and I was completely fine with the sort of straight line stuff. But it was when I was having to turn to come off lines, like in

a beep test, or a yo-yo test, I was getting that pain back. That's when I realised that it wasn't just a little tweak.'

George reported his injury to the Rugby Academy staff,

'When I told them it was an injury that's come from athletics, they were a bit angry about it. Because they expect their players not to do anything in the off-season. So when you come to pre-season and you say, 'I've got injured from athletics', they think that athletics is like quite a trivial thing and it's kind of like you're doing it for a bit of fun and especially if they don't know who you are in athletics. They can kind of overlook it.'

George began treatment. The National Schools Championships were only two weeks away and he had to compete.

'He's (the physio) being really cautious with it, because he knows that a groin injury can come back and every time it comes back, it comes back worse.'

Finally George got the all clear and was given a date to return to full training. The only problem was that the Schools Championships were to be held the Friday before! George explained to the physio how important the Championships were to him. The physio said that it was his decision and he would have to *'suffer the consequences.'*

George knew the club was:

'Quite hostile towards athletics. They just

didn't understand what sort of competition it was and it's not one of those things you want to miss.'

But George was always going to go.

THE NATIONAL SCHOOLS CHAMPIONSHIPS

George knew that if he threw at his best he would win, but he hadn't been able to throw for 10 days going into the competition. Normally he could deal with pressure really well.

'But it's when I put pressure on myself, that's when I normally struggle.'

He threw two no throws in his first two attempts in the final and watched as his closest rival took the lead with a throw of 52.07m, a new personal best. George was really nervous. His groin was holding up but he knew that he couldn't force it. He just needed to relax, keep his technique together and make one big throw.

George launched the discus.

'Normally a discus thrower can tell as soon as you've released it, if it's going to be a good throw. You look up and you can normally tell if it's a good throw and you get feedback from yourself, you actually feel like you've thrown it quite far.'

George threw 56.26m!

Just when it mattered, he had pulled it off. First place was his. He had finally achieved his goal after striving for it for three years, and even better was to come. Next week he would get to represent his country at the Schools Athletics Internationals.

But first it was back to rugby!

BACK TO RUGBY

Back at rugby training, George checked in with the physio. He told him his groin was fine and then went to join the others.

'I'd just warmed up and the Academy Director came over and said, 'Can I have a chat with you?' So we went upstairs and he pretty much just gave me a bollocking.

He said that I was an okay rugby player which pretty much means average, and that my athletics was much better. Even though out of all the lads in my age group down at the Academy there were only three of us that had played for our country.

But I was still just an okay rugby player in his eyes.

He asked me what I thought, but then he just continued. He spoke about the club's ethos, saying I was undermining the club by doing athletics.

All I could do was just sit there and think. Like the club doesn't do anything for me, they don't pay me, there's no sort of like financial or any support whatsoever. It's like I come to training, you turn me into a rugby player. I don't think so! They don't really have any sort of like legal control over what I do. But I just had to sit there and listen to it for about twenty minutes.

Then he actually said that for my punish-

ment I wasn't going to train......for that day. So I came in for the warmup and then got told, 'I want you to go home now.'

I was probably just angry really. Angry and just a bit disappointed in the club. I'd given them so much over the last three years, and tried to juggle both sports and tried to do it as best I could, but that wasn't good enough for them. As far as they were concerned, doing both didn't work.

I pretty much just finished what I was doing and then got a lift home.

I didn't feel like I deserved punishment .... There wasn't a need for them to bollock me about it at all.'

TIME TO CHOOSE

Two days later, George went back to the Academy with his Mum for a meeting.

'At that meeting the Academy Director pretty much gave me the ultimatum of 'You're gonna have to pick rugby or athletics. One of them.'

George thought about it. He was getting tired of trying to do both and giving 50% to each. He was never going to get really good at either if he kept trying to focus on both at the same time.

'The Academy Director kind of seemed like he wanted me to make the decision to go down the athletics route. By saying I was an okay rugby player and that my athletics was like up here and my rugby was all the way down here. So when he *was talking about it, it seemed that he wanted me to make the decision to go down the athletics route.*

Prior to that point I hadn't decided, but in the lead-up, all the way through pre-season it felt like there had been a massive hostility towards athletics. And rugby wasn't a very nice atmosphere, especially when you're training in a really intense environment like that. You want to enjoy being there, because it's not easy, and you don't want to be somewhere where you don't actually like being. I think pretty much after that meeting I'd already made up in my mind that my relationship with them was pretty much done now.'

George was right and his prediction that '*I think something is going to happen that makes me choose one of them*' had come true.

The sad reality was that George was still enjoying his rugby '*just as much*' as his athletics. He hadn't actually made a decision to stop playing rugby and he hadn't picked rugby over athletics, he had just decided that he couldn't carry on where he was anymore.

George was then selected as a 17-year-old to represent his country at the European Athletics Under 20 Championships in Sweden. He qualified for the final and finished in a creditable 10th position.

The Championships were on the same day that George's school rugby team set off on their pre-season tour. While he was no longer a member of a professional Rugby Academy, he could still play for his school. This was a trip that George was never going to miss. The night the Championships finished, he flew from Sweden to Johannesburg to catch up with the touring party. George hadn't decided to stop playing rugby, he had just decided that from now on, he would play on his own terms.

'I still enjoy my rugby just as much as my athletics at the moment. I'm loving playing for school and I'd like to try (and) get down the national route again.'

Maybe rugby shouldn't have given up on him!

SPORT SPECIALISATION

KEY TAKEAWAYS

Sport specialisation is intensive, year-round training and participation in a single sport (as opposed to a diversified approach where a person trains and participates in more than one sport).

When young children first start to play sport, the primary influences on their continued participation are their level of enjoyment and perceived ability. If young children participate in a range of sports, then there is more chance that they will stay engaged and find the sport they enjoy the most. Young children want to play, have fun and enjoy learning. Support for their sport sampling is vital to this process.

Sport sampling not only facilitates the development of a wider range of physical and psychological skills. It is also associated with a decreased risk of sports injury. When a child feels competent in their sport, then their confidence and motivation will grow. They will be much more likely to keep playing and enjoying sport.

When participation in more than one sport is sustained over the longer term, each young person gradually finds this situation more difficult to manage. Eventually, teenagers need to reduce their number of participation sports. For the talented athlete, continued participation will no longer have the same association with enjoyment. Instead, their motivation to improve and excel will become their primary driver. Late sport specialisation offers an athlete greater potential for long-term success in their chosen sport. It enables him or her to draw from and build upon a broader base of physical, technical and mental skills.

George's experience reveals the potential downside of the power dynamic within the talent development environment and demonstrates how it is crucial for the objectives of the coach and athlete to align. The key to effective collaboration is the coach's ability to create conditions that promote each individual athlete's engagement. The irony in the environment created by sports talent development programs is that they actively search to identify unique athletes, and then require those individuals to conform to a common set of standards and expectations.

As the talent development process progresses, it is important that the athlete and coach learn not only how to communicate but also how to negotiate. The young athlete is best served when both coaches and parents learn to listen and respond appropriately to their views on issues that affect their participation and performance.

TALENT DEVELOPMENT TIPS

◆ Support young athletes to progress in the sport that is right for them.

This requires parents to provide their sons and daughters with the opportunity to try different sports, and when the time is right, coaches need to find ways to support their athletes to effectively transition their focus to a single sport.

◆ Treat talent development as a shared relationship between coach, athlete and parents.

Everyone in the relationship should invest in positive communication and be prepared to negotiate.

◆ Respect that each talented athlete is a unique individual.

Strive to preserve each athlete's individuality, rather than expecting him or her to behave like everyone else.

CHAPTER 2

IDENTITY

In this chapter, you will gain insights into how:

- ◆ A positive talent development experience relies upon personalised and holistic athlete development.
- ◆ To help a young athlete to keep the significance of sports participation and performance in context.
- ◆ To avoid a sport-dominated narrative.

EBONI'S STORY

TWO WORLDS COLLIDE

Eboni has been playing netball for five years. She started playing for school when she was 12 years old and at 13 she played for her District and County. At 14, Eboni was selected for the regional side and then promoted to the National Talent League Development Squad. At club level, she played for the Under 16s when she was just 14 and her team made it all the way to the national finals.

> 'We trained a lot to get there.'

Last year her club team missed out on the nationals but this year it was *'the strongest it has ever been'* and they qualified again. They were to be held during an important time at school for Eboni – exam week – but this was her last chance to go to the national finals and she wanted to be there.

COUNTDOWN

Eboni was really busy. The national finals were just two weeks away but at that moment *'it was all exams'*. She was still supposed to be training with the regional squad and the regional coach didn't like anyone to miss sessions, so each player had to send her their eight-week schedule.

> *'All our training, all our extra training, all our revision times and all our exam timetables as well. It took ages, it took like three hours to fill out with the details she wanted.'*

That helped though because now there was:

> *'Less regional training. I think she's decided if it's too close to an exam then we don't have to come in, but we can't miss all of them obviously.'*

Especially with the school work because:

The Young Athlete's Perspective

'Your parents are telling you to revise. There's a lot more pressure. You have to have good time management around this time, definitely.'

Eboni was focused on her exams. She hadn't had time to even think about the nationals.

'I think the career side and netball side is completely different in my head. That is like two different worlds to me.'

But last night at training the kit was given out and now it was starting to feel real. It was getting close. All of a sudden Eboni felt like she was under pressure.

'A lot more pressure.'

'NETBALL FIRST'

Last night the club coach told them that she had added in three more training sessions.

Around six exams! They added one on Wednesday and they added on one for next Wednesday, but I had two exams like the day, the night before, the night after! So I'm just struggling to get revision in.'

The pressure was mounting. Exams were bad enough, but now the coaches were making it worse. She talked to the other girls about it.

Yeah we talk about it a lot I think.
Last night, 'cause we've all had our history exam today......and a lot of girls had the PE exam in the afternoon. So I think we were just talking

about how much work we got and I think some of them had ten exams this week and then they were doing like double the training.'

They had thought about missing a regional session but that wasn't going to be easy with her regional coach's attitude either.

'Cause I think she wasn't very happy with the fact that we'd missed one anyway. She'd already had words with us. 'Cause she was saying…like, 'If you want to progress in the program and get further in this level, then you have to come to the next few sessions…..or next year will be very difficult.' And things like that.'

'She kind of knows we have exams but still expects us to go. So if we had an exam on the Friday, but we had weight training on Wednesday, she'd expect us to be there. But she still might expect us to go for an hour on the Wednesday, if the exam is on a Thursday for example.'

'Netball's first' is her favourite phrase.

So it's a lot of pressure I think, when she says things like that.'

Eboni's club coach wasn't as bad as that though, she was more relaxed.

'She doesn't tend to shout at us very often, but she expects us to be at training all the time.

And even if we're injured, we're expected to be at the training.'

NATIONALS WEEKEND

Eboni's team came fourth at the nationals. Being a

member of the fourth-best Under 16 club team in the country was a great way for her to end junior netball. It was a really good achievement, especially considering they had gone to the nationals without their coach.

> 'It wasn't our usual coach, 'cause our usual coach is pregnant and I think she had the baby this week when we were down there.'

FAIR PLAY

Eboni had a really good time at the nationals. She was picked to start and got plenty of time, but she was well aware that that wasn't the case for everyone. Twelve girls made the travelling team but:

> 'Some girls didn't even get picked to go down.'

And of the twelve who did go:

> 'Some girls didn't get to play.'

Eboni thought about the other girls.

> 'I went down with one of my best friends and she only got a quarter for the weekend.
> I think she enjoyed it anyway, but you don't really talk about it. You don't say, 'You didn't really get played that much.' It's not really a conversation anyone has.'

But Eboni did have a particular view on that, and she didn't see it the same as the coach.

> 'I think to begin with she put the strongest team out, which I would have agreed with. 'Cause you don't know what the teams are like. But

when it got to the third quarter and we're miles ahead.........and there's no way we could lose like by that much in a third quarter. You bring on other players, try different combinations for other matches.

So there would have been (a) chance to do that if she had wanted to. Yeah definitely and if we had lost it by a ridiculous amount and you want to get it back again, you put your strongest team back on for the fourth quarter. That's how I would have thought to do it. But instead she kept the strongest team, like the main team on.........for most of the matches.'

SENIOR NETBALL

There was no Under 18 side at Eboni's club, so she had to trial for the Seniors if she wanted to stay on after the juniors. That was really hard because now she had to compete against professional Super League netballers just to stay at her own club.

Eboni came through the trial though and now she was in a squad of 30 to 40 players. This brought a new dynamic. It was a much higher standard but although the competition was tough, some things were just the same.

'It has kicked off a bit with club.

No one was turning up to training because everyone does so much training (which) clashes with other things.

Yes, so it clashes with the Super League, a lot of girls got into the national side this year so if they have a national camp at the weekend, they

The Young Athlete's Perspective

are only allowed to play three hours a week leading up to the camp, and after as well, so they have half an hour in training then they leave.

So then no one is coming to training and I think they (the coaches) were really annoyed because at one point, they couldn't get a squad out for a game. That meant they had to forfeit the game, which cost the club money and obviously a reputation thing.

So then we had our head coach, who is a big Super League manager and coach as well, come in to try and shout at all of us saying 'Why were you not in training, why are you not turning up for matches?' and things like that.

There is a three-strike system so if you miss three training sessions in the year, then you are out of the club completely. The issue was that everyone who was there being shouted at are the people who are there every single week, and people who weren't there being shouted at were the people who needed to be shouted at.

Most of us come into training all the time.'

PLANNING AHEAD

Eboni still lives in two worlds, and she is still working hard at getting better at netball but:

'I don't think I'd ever go national level or Super League or professional like that.'

At school, Eboni is studying for her final exams and:

'It is a lot more, it is harder and the exams which I didn't realise how much I had to revise.

Usually I would revise the week leading up and I'd be fine, but I can see the difference definitely. But it is fine, I just need to manage my time even more now so if I have got a spare hour, I can't just chill out, I just need to actually do work.'

Just lately one of the teachers has been a little concerned about Eboni's workload:

'So she said, 'Write out your schedule for me', which I did, and she said 'It was a bit ridiculous' and 'Was I thinking about dropping a subject?'

But I just said, 'No, because I want my four subjects!'

Eboni has a plan. She is headed to university and she knows what she wants to study.

'Human rights law.'

Eboni's two worlds may have more in common than she realises!

IDENTITY

KEY TAKEAWAYS

Adolescents consider sport to be part of their identity, and that sports participation provides a sense of social belonging and allows them to be themselves. However, while sports participation has the potential to connect, engage and empower the young athlete, their identity does not have to be directly linked to their success in sport. Learning this is essential to their health and wellbeing.

Young people learn and develop through interaction with both their social and physical environments. During adolescence, their brains are moulded by their experiences and relationships. The adolescent pursuit of an identity relies upon the development of relationships and the process of becoming part of a particular social world. It also relies on the development of an independence that is achieved by separating from others.

Adolescence is a time when the young person seeks support from friends through mutual activities and the sharing of common interests to create an independent identity. Sports participation (and in particular, involvement in a sport talent development program) can play a significant role in this process. Young athletes are greatly influenced by how they believe their identity is perceived by others and so will modify their behaviour to safeguard and promote their positive reputation.

However, while different athletes will have different motivation to pursue sporting excellence at different times, ultimately this time will end for all of them. Supportive parents and coaches must always acknowledge this reality and consistently encourage the holistic development of their young athletes. This can be done by supporting them to develop positive identities by pursuing their ambitions in areas outside of sport. It is essential for parents and coaches to encourage all athletes to continue to be (and see themselves as) much more than athletes.

TALENT DEVELOPMENT TIPS

◆ A positive talent development experience relies upon personalised and holistic athlete development.

    Take the time to recognise effort and achievement, celebrate personal milestones and value the young athlete's diverse transitions both inside and outside of sport.

◆ Help a young athlete to keep the significance of sports participation and performance in context.

    Emphasise the importance of hard work, aspiration and ambition in other important areas of their life like education and employment.

◆ Avoid a sport-dominated narrative.

    Enable the creation of a multi-dimensional identity by encouraging the young athlete to pursue outside interests and explore different opportunities. Value and reinforce the importance of their time spent away from sport with family and friends.

CHAPTER 3

GROWTH, MATURATION, HEALTH AND WELLBEING

In this chapter, you will gain insights into:

- How to guide the young athlete through competing physical demands and psychological challenges.
- Why young athletes can have a greater risk of injuries and may suffer dips in form during adolescence.
- Why young athletes may mask injuries in misguided attempts to safeguard their reputations in the eyes of their coaches.

DAN'S STORY

STANDING STILL BUT MOVING FORWARDS

Dan started playing badminton for fun with his family when he was nine years old, and now he is 17. By the age of 10 he was on the performance pathway training three times a week, and by 13 he was up to five times a week.

Dan was training hard and making progress. By 14, he was competing in the men's league. He wanted to make the top three in his grade and he had a gold ranking in his sights. (Grades reflect a player's ability and higher-graded players can enter Gold tournaments.) Dan's goal was to become a professional badminton player.

At 15, Dan was injured. He had developed patella tendinopathy.

His coaches told him to take it easy, but Dan wanted to play on. He thought that he didn't need to stop – he could play through it and so play on he did. He continued training and playing five days a week. Playing in the men's league was tough and each game would cause him quite a bit of pain, but he still carried on.

Dan didn't really know what was wrong, he just thought it would go away. His coaches had left it up to him to sort it out, but it was getting harder. He couldn't cover the court, his knee felt like it was giving way. The pain was eight out of 10 and the more he played, the worse it got.

It was becoming a real struggle and he was frustrated. Other players were catching up to him. He knew he had to make progress. He was better than them, but he couldn't move. Finally, he went to the doctor. They told him he needed to stop and rest.

TREATMENT PLAN

Dan wanted to get back to play as soon as possible, so he did exactly what the doctor said. First it was rest and ice, but that didn't work. Next he saw a physio who gave him exercises. Dan tried his best and did the exercises, but they were painful. He needed to strengthen his leg but he could see his muscles were wasting away. The treatment wasn't helping, and he still couldn't play.

Dan thought about what he could do in his down time. There was a badminton coaching course, so he signed up. He was 16 and everyone else on the course was older, but that didn't put him off. He got some new ideas and learnt about different tactics. He thought it was good to be able to understand where you might have gone wrong in a match and he learnt how to analyse his game.

Meanwhile, badminton continued without him. It was time for the qualifying rounds for the nationals. His doubles partner Mark couldn't wait any longer; he found a new partner. That was tough, Mark was his friend. They went to school together, they had known each other since first year and became friends through playing together. Now they were more than just badminton friends. They saw each other every day. Mark told Dan about everything he was missing.

The weeks had rolled on but the treatment hadn't worked. Next they wanted Dan to try dry needling, then after two weeks he could try doing some *'really light sport'* in five-minute blocks. Dan hadn't played at all in the last six months, and maybe it was longer. Finally, now he could try again.

He arranged to meet Mark to play some *'light bad-*

minton'. He went back on court, but it was still painful!

'Maybe it was bruising from the needle,' he thought to himself. *'Yes that's probably what it was.'*

It was hard to stick to five minutes, so he carried on a little longer. He played some good shots, he still had it! But he wasn't really moving. His friend was *'feeding him'* shots. He couldn't put his weight through his left leg. It was too soon, it was still painful.

SMALL STEPS

Dan wasn't going to give up. He was determined to get back playing. He went back to the physio. He got new exercises and he did them every day. He tried playing a little longer, but was his injury improving? Now the pain was more like a five or six out of 10, so he did think it was. He still couldn't move around quickly but he could play, just not like before. He needed more time and he knew that if he changed his game and played more defensive shots, then it could help buy him the time to recover. He had to be careful landing and pushing off, so he adjusted his technique to take two steps instead of one:

'Everything just took slightly longer.'

Dan wasn't ready to go back to the talent development program, but at least now he had a way to get back playing again. He practised with Mark and he practised against Mark. He still wasn't 100%. He knew he could play a lot better, but he was playing and he enjoyed it. Now he wasn't trying to get better, he just wanted to play, he could get better when his knee was right.

Dan was 17 now. He had been in pain for two years, so he wasn't going to rush things. The one thing he didn't want to do now was make it worse.

MOVING ON

Dan had been told that he could go back to the talent development program as soon as he was fit. Now his knee was much better. The pain had gone out of his mind and the physio had discharged him. He had done everything he could to try and get back, but it had taken two years.

Dan finally recognised that wanting to be a badminton player was now past tense. When people talked about badminton, they didn't talk about him anymore. He didn't know how it had happened, but things had moved on.

He had exams now anyway (his finals), so he needed to revise. He wanted to study biology, life was no longer all about badminton for him. Dan was focused on the future and planning for university.

He still loved badminton and once he got to uni he was sure he would play, but for now he needed to get good grades. He was studying hard and that was his priority. His future looked bright, but his future wasn't in badminton.

GROWTH, MATURATION, HEALTH AND WELLBEING

KEY TAKEAWAYS

Individual athlete age and stage of development should always be a key consideration in talent development. Adolescence is the developmental stage when a person's final growth spurt occurs. The period within adolescence when the maximum rate of growth occurs is known as 'peak height velocity' (PHV). This happens at around 12-15 years of age for males and 11-14 for females.

Young athletes who are chronologically older within their age group and/or more mature can have a comparative performance advantage which often leads to developmental opportunities. This advantage is known as the 'relative age effect' (RAE) and explains why a relatively older athlete is more likely to be selected for (and to progress within) a talent development program.

The talent development environment introduces the young athlete to training and competition at increasing levels of volume and intensity. The downside is that an increased focus on the acquisition and development of sport-specific skills during puberty coincides with the athlete's major growth spurt, and he or she is then exposed to a significantly higher risk of injury.

This period can also be accompanied by a phenomenon termed 'adolescent awkwardness', where changes in neurology and stature present the athlete with coordination challenges that may temporarily hinder progress and performance.

Dan's story demonstrates early but unsustainable

progress. By 14 he was competing in the men's league, but by 15 he was suffering from an overuse injury. Now when he reflects he confesses:

> 'That was probably the reason why I got the injury because I was playing too much.'

His story demonstrates the potential power of the young athlete's desires, beliefs and attitudes to influence their behaviour in a way that can put their future wellbeing at risk. Playing with an injury or making a premature return to play after one can have long-term effects. Another example of how this scenario can play out for a young athlete is explained below:

> *Yes, my coach knew I had an injury. He said to me before, 'If it hurts don't do it, but don't use it as an excuse not to do it,' and from that I took it well I'm going to have to do it then...............I could feel it in the session, but I just kept running because of what he said. I probably made it worse. If you want to impress the coach, then you don't want to say, 'Oh I'm injured, can I drop out?', you just want to keep playing because you don't want to look silly not doing it.'*

This example highlights how psychology can negatively influence an adolescent athlete's decision-making and behaviour to cause injuries or make them worse. It's not just their training load during their growth spurt that can be problematic in terms of injuries. Their actions may be governed not by what the coach says, but by a motivation to safeguard their reputation in the eyes of the coach.

> *'You're pretty much talking to the guys that*

are gonna decide whether you're gonna become a professional player or not. So you don't want to say anything that's gonna put you in a bad spot with them really.'

Young people in a talent development environment learn to adjust their behaviour to conform to the expectations and values of other important people in the group where they want to belong. A coach is obviously an important person in a talent development group. When injured or ill in this environment, the athlete will not want to risk conveying a negative impression to the coach.

However, if the coach can guide athletes through this time, a trusting relationship can be established. Through increased collaboration, these athletes can then find ways to positively influence their practice and individualise their learning to help ensure their long-term health and wellbeing.

TALENT DEVELOPMENT TIPS

- Guide the young athlete through competing physical demands and psychological challenges.

    Reassure the athlete that non-linear development is a normal part of the developmental process. Athletes, coaches and parents all need to recognise the influence of relative age effects and to understand the necessity of individualised athlete development plans.

- Young athletes can have a greater risk of injuries and may suffer dips in form during adolescence.

    Monitor an adolescent athlete's growth spurt, maturity and activity, and adjust his or her training exposure accordingly. Rest and recovery are essential to a growing athlete and the young athlete should not try to please everybody.

- Young athletes may mask injuries in misguided attempts to safeguard their reputations in the eyes of their coaches.

    A young athlete must learn to manage competing demands and be guided to make decisions that prioritise their long-term health and wellbeing.

Graham Turner

CHAPTER 4

SELF-PRESENTATION

In this chapter, you will gain insights into:

- Why optimal athlete and coach collaboration relies upon a genuine relationship and authentic communication.
- How a talent development program is designed to develop the individual athlete, not the team.
- Why the aim of a talent development program is to promote the uniqueness of the individual.

ROWAN'S STORY

YOU'VE GOT TO BELIEVE

Rowan is 15 years old and he is a rugby player on the national performance pathway in the UK. He started life as a footballer (soccer player) and he started to learn about talent development programs when he was eight.

EARLY LEARNING

> 'I got released from a professional club at the end of Under 8's. Then I was just like, really nervous because I didn't know what to do when I got released. I was like, do I go back and play or do I just stop because I feel like I'm being told that I'm rubbish and I don't deserve to do it?'

When Rowan was 10 he switched from football to rugby, and at age 11 he was invited on to a rugby talent development program. He is progressing well in the Rugby Academy (junior development squad) at a professional club.

> 'I want to become a professional rugby player, so I'm going to do everything I can to become a professional rugby player.'

Rowan explained that the expectations in the club's talent development program are clear.

> 'We always know that they are looking to recruit, they are looking to let go.'

When I asked him how he felt about this, he said:

> 'Yes it gets you slightly worried, it does get to you.'

But Rowan has learnt how to cope with it. The Academy have taught him that:

> 'You've just got to believe in yourself.'

THE YOUNG ATHLETE'S PERSPECTIVE

BELIEVING IN YOURSELF!

Rowan plays for the *'best club'* in the area. This year they won the cup final where they *'hammered'* the opposition. The talent development program is going well and the coaches have told him that he just needs to keep heading in the same direction.

One coach has told him that if he keeps progressing he could be the number one player in the county in his age group. Another told him that if he puts his mind to it he can make it. He knows that:

> *'It is not very often that people get told that.'*

At school Rowan has been picked to play for the year above his age group.

> *'It is an honour to me because I am a year below and they are such a good rugby year and they've got so many players to choose from. They've already got a player in my position, so to go as a 9 to play for them in the Cup and in Sevens, I was over the moon.'*

The Head of the Academy has said that he is very pleased with Rowan. They can see him developing and they think there is a bright future ahead for him if he keeps going the way he is.

Rowan's cousin is also at the club. He *'is at a very high stage in rugby'* and that's good for Rowan because he tells him what he needs to do and helps him practise. His cousin has told him that the coaches *'look for a hard trainer, because a hard trainer looks like a player that is committed to the sport and wants to learn,'* so Rowan makes sure that he is always at the front, even in the warmups.

This year the Academy coaches have been suitably impressed with Rowan and they have decided that he doesn't need to go to the District Trial. He can go straight to the final County Trial instead.

'I am nominating myself as a scrum half because I know that I've probably got one of the best passes.'

Rowan understands what the coaches want. He knows they only want the best players and he is determined to show everyone around him that he is the best.

'It is about me, I can focus on other people, but if I see someone getting better than me, or see someone creeping up behind me that's when I start to go uphill. I don't get phased by anyone that I see who is having a better game than me. I just think yes he's had a better game than me, I'm going to accept it but then next time I'm going to show him and just make sure he knows that I'm there and not that he is just going to walk his way through.'

Rowan is confident in his ability and confident in his coach's belief in his ability.

'There is not much competition at 9, there is one who is small, (and) skinny and then there is one other who plays at ******* and coaches don't rate him really.'

He also knows how to play like a good player.

'Being a scrum half you have to be vocal. Some players don't like when I'm like that but I can't help it. Everybody else and the good play-

ers understand that and they don't mind. It's the players that aren't too good that don't like that.'

And if another player represents a threat, then he knows how to deal with it.

'When I see my opposition player in the game, I just watch what he is doing. One of the teams we play against has a tricky little 9 but he doesn't have a kick, so that's what I try to notice. I use my kick to put him in positions where he has to kick. So I try and make him look bad compared to me.'

MAKING PROGRESS

Last year was a good year for Rowan. In the summer, the Academy asked him to train with the year above and he played his first game against another professional club side.

'I was so pleased, being an underage player and getting an opportunity. It was something that I've always wanted to do, play for my home town, I got about 25 to 30 minutes. The opposition were a big strong side. I mean some of the boys must have been about six foot and weigh about 100kg which is scary. I just remember stepping on the pitch and just thinking, is this actually happening? Because I didn't know what was going on at first but it was an amazing experience.'

Now Rowan has the chance to get to know the scrum half in the age group above him and that's been really useful for him.

'Keep your friends close, but keep your enemies closer. He's not really an enemy but he is someone that I am opposing against so I've just got to make sure that he knows I'm there. So when he passes a distance, I'll try to beat his distance. He doesn't stand out to me, he doesn't do things, he doesn't believe in himself much.'

This year Rowan wants to be the first choice 9 for the County. Two teams will be picked, but for Rowan it's *'A's or nothing.'* He's confident and he believes he can do it.

'I love playing in pressure because that is when I play at my best. That is when I perform.'

Everything is going great. Rowan is going to be a rugby player and he can feel it getting *'nearer and nearer'*.

WOULD YOU BELIEVE IT?

It was just a normal game. Then 10 minutes into the second half, Rowan tackled a player running down the wing. They both fell awkwardly. The winger came down on top of Rowan and landed right on his thumb. Instantly there was a sharp *'nasty pain'*.

Rowan got up and tried to carry on playing but he knew something was wrong. He threw a pass and watched as the ball bounced on the turf. The next one was the same. His passing was off. He looked down at his thumb, it was hurting and it was swollen. He knew he'd done something but he had to play on.

Back home after the game he got out the ice. He couldn't even pull the door open. It hurt. It hurt a lot. The next day was Sunday, so he knew if he rested it, his thumb would settle down. The day after that was training. Maybe if he got it strapped it would be alright?

The physio checked it and strapped it up. It didn't seem too bad but the physio said it was best not to train. By Thursday Rowan had had enough. It was still hurting a lot. He needed to go to hospital and get it checked.

Finally the doctor came back with the results. Rowan's worst fears were confirmed. The X-ray showed a fracture and he was out of action. Rowan was really annoyed but he was determined to get back as quickly as possible.

Six weeks later Rowan's plaster cast was off and he was ready to go back to training.

'How does it feel Rowan' I asked?

'It feels perfect' he replied.

'Perfect?' I asked again.

'I mean it's not pain free, like I can push against there and I've still got a bit of a niggle on the outside of the bone, but it is alright.'

The Doctor had told Rowan that his thumb would need to be strapped and that it would have to be strapped forever, but Rowan was going to be a rugby player and the Academy had taught him that you had to believe in yourself. If Rowan said his thumb was perfect, then it would be.

Graham Turner

SELF-PRESENTATION

KEY TAKEAWAYS

Self-presentation in the talent development context refers to the behaviours that young athletes display in an attempt to control the impressions that influential others form about them. These behaviours are based on their desire to achieve their personal goals.

Talent identification focuses on a young athlete's ability and potential. A commodity status may be conferred on these athletes. Talent development programs only commit to each young athlete for as long as their talent trajectory is maintained.

Young athletes in talent development programs learn that their futures will be determined by the impression they make on the adults who control their specific programs. They subsequently develop a distinct consciousness of what it is like to be continually judged and they learn to exist in a reality where they are always on trial.

These young athletes not only learn to look for when they are being watched, but they also learn to make judgements about the relative importance of what is being watched, and who is watching. It soon becomes clear that their continued existence in their programs is dependent upon their ability to interpret and respond to the wishes of their coaches. No matter how difficult life becomes, they learn to not question his or her authority.

Continual evaluation is a critical component of the talent development process in sport. Young people's motivation to use self-presentational behaviour changes with age as they begin to recognise that using self-promotional tactics can influence people's judgement of their competence.

Self-presentation therefore is a deliberate attempt to project personal skills and attributes with the goal of creating the most positive impression. This type of behaviour is often expressed differently by boys. Girls may be less likely to self-promote and more likely to use less overt self-presentation styles.

The young athlete's self-presentational behaviour will be modified based on what he or she believes to be the goals of the coach. This can result in a disconnect between what the coach expects (or is looking for) and what the athlete *believes* the coach is *really* looking for.

This potential for a disconnect underlines the importance of the coach having the ability to clearly guide the athlete's expectations. This can be achieved by providing regular constructive feedback that focuses on individual athlete needs and personal challenges.

TALENT DEVELOPMENT TIPS

- Optimal athlete and coach collaboration relies upon a genuine relationship and authentic communication.

    The coach must be aware of the messages they send and seek when communicating with the athlete. This includes asking for input and working to understand and incorporate the young person's point of view.

- The talent development program is designed to develop the individual athlete, not the team.

    Benchmark the athlete's progress against national standards and expectations rather than through peer comparison.

- The aim of the talent development program is to promote the uniqueness of the individual.

    Encourage each young athlete to believe in his or her ability, to continue to be different and not to lose sight of what has brought success. Know what sets him or her apart from other young athletes.

CHAPTER 5

SELF-DETERMINATION

In this chapter, you will gain insights into:

- ◆ How, autonomy, connectedness and a sense of competence are critical to the young athlete's motivation.
- ◆ The importance of providing each athlete with positive options.
- ◆ Why it is the athlete who decides how long he or she continues on the performance pathway.

LAURA'S STORY

FINDING A WAY

Laura is 15 and she has been a gymnast for 11 years. Each year she competes in the national clubs regional qualifier. The top four placed gymnasts qualify for the national final.

Graham Turner

A DIFFICULT LIFE

Each training night, Laura gets straight into her parent's car after school and sets off for the gym. There is never any time to spare. She grabs a sandwich, eats it on the way and has just enough time to get changed and be ready before training begins. She trains five times a week. Training is hard and lasts for three and a half hours.

When Laura gets home it's too late to do homework. She's tired and needs to sleep. Each morning she gets to school early because she has to keep on top of her work.

Weekend training sessions are longer and harder. Four hours on Saturday and four hours on Sunday. There is no let up, life is difficult.

Laura has been training like this since she was seven years old and she has known most of her coaches since then. Helen is a really good coach in terms of bringing on the younger gymnasts. Laura used to really like her, but as she got older her relationships with all her coaches became different. It was like the coaches just didn't know how to deal with teenagers.

As each year went by, training got harder. More and more of Laura's friends had dropped out and now there were hardly any older gymnasts left. Helen didn't know how to coach teenagers and she didn't know how to deal with them. That's why they quit. They had tried to tell her, but it was like they just kept having the same conversation over and over again.

In the end, they couldn't be bothered anymore. Helen got upset about it but she didn't listen and nothing changed. She still spoke to Laura like she was a child and now, if she was honest, Laura really didn't like her.

The Young Athlete's Perspective

When Laura was nine, John started to coach her. John was a good coach and some of his gymnasts had really gone far over the years. John shouted at you, and when John shouted, you did it. But now Laura was older, shouting didn't work anymore. Now when John shouted it had the opposite effect. Laura didn't want to follow his instructions at all.

He used to be good but now he didn't know how to motivate her and it seemed like he couldn't be bothered anyway. He was *'getting old'* and he was *'getting lazy'*. He wasn't at all the training sessions and that made it difficult because when he wasn't, Laura had to go back to Helen. Laura preferred a male coach.

'Because I'm quite tall as a gymnast and she is smaller than me, so if I'm doing something quite difficult and if I need support for it, it is quite hard because she is not bigger physically. So it is difficult when I have to train with her because I won't do anything, it's like if I need support I just refuse to do anything if she is there.'

CRISIS OF CONFIDENCE

Laura was preparing for a national competition. She had two weeks to go, but she was worried and thinking of pulling out. She hadn't told her coaches or her parents. She wanted to compete but she had a problem with one of her tumbles. She wasn't confident she could pull it off. In training she had kept trying and trying, but it just hadn't gone well.

The nationals had made her nervous last time as well. It wasn't just the shaking, she was nervous inside and her belly felt really funny. That time she had decided to go for it and just try her best. She started well. After vault and bars, she was coming fourth, but then it was time for floor. Laura had thought about the tumble in her warmup. *'Should she have one last practice?'* She decided against it. There was no point now, it wasn't going to change.

The music started..
She got to the tumble and she went for it ....and then she fell, just like she knew she would. She always fell on the landing.

Laura ended up with a really low score. She beat herself up for days. She was:

'Really, really upset and annoyed.'

She didn't even know why she was there. It was very upsetting. She would always be annoyed about it.

Laura knew that her coaches always thought she was going to be really good when she was younger.

'When I was seven, I'd just do whatever I was asked or at least try.'

Now they were trying to make her learn a load of new and difficult skills, but Laura was scared and she wouldn't do them. The problem was that her coaches just didn't understand how difficult some things were for her.

But Laura still had two weeks to go to this year's nationals.

'I'm not ready. I don't want to compete, but my coach is just not helping. I'm getting scared of

The Young Athlete's Perspective

doing stuff that I shouldn't be scared of doing and instead of helping me get it back, he'll just shout at me and say, 'You should be able to do that' and things like that, so I have to actually get my other friends to help me do it because he won't do it.

It's hard, I don't know whether to carry on or not.'

Laura wanted to train by herself and just do what she needed to do without other people watching. She wanted to practise without anyone thinking what she was doing was stupid, and not have her coach shouting at her. Just a day where she could be by herself. She had ideas but her coaches never listened to them. They just tried to make her perform the skills. She wanted to leave.

'But I don't know where else I could go.'

Laura knew she had the ability to learn the new skills, but mentally she was too scared. If only club training was like squad training. Squad training was at a different gym and they had pits there. Laura liked squad training because she knew she could somersault into the pit there and wasn't going to hurt herself.

But her club gym didn't have facilities like that, so it was difficult to learn new skills. Even if she could do it, she was scared because when she got it wrong it hurt; like the other day when she was somersaulting on vault. She didn't tuck in tight enough so she didn't get round, landing awkwardly on her foot and whacking her finger. She couldn't move it afterwards, it was really swollen.

Now she had a problem with beam.

'When I think about what I am doing, it scares me and that is when I lose stuff and I won't

do stuff.'

It was on her mind all the time. John had tried to help, but he hadn't really done much.

'I don't really think he cares.'

Laura was on her own. It was up to her to find a way. She knew that if she kept on practising she could eventually get it, but she was running out of time. She didn't know how she would do it, but she was determined to do it.

'I knew I'd do everything on the day, so I just said, 'I'm going to compete'.'

COMPETITION DAY

Laura felt really sick on the day of the comp. She fell off the beam and she fell again during floor, this time on her easiest tumble. She was concerned about one of her main rivals.

'I actually thought that she was beating me by quite a bit and after floor I thought she was going to win, because I didn't realise I was winning on beam because I fell off and she didn't. I assumed that she was winning when she wasn't. I won beam and then after floor she was almost a mark ahead of me, but then my vault was really good compared to her so then my coach pulled me aside and told me that she was only 0.3 ahead. If I didn't muck up my bar routine, I could win.'

But deep down, Laura thought she would fall off on her bar routine.

'I knew I was going to fall off on that because it wasn't going right in warmup, and then the girl before me, she fell off, so my coach just said, 'Just leave it out, and I stuck my bar routine and that is why I won!'

A NEW WAY FORWARD

Laura felt really good winning the comp, but winning wasn't enough for her. She still wanted to get really good. She thought about changing clubs but that wasn't the answer because she didn't want to leave her friends. Laura needed to keep going, she knew that her coaches could be *'quite difficult people'* but now she could see a potential new way forward. There was a chance to start working with a different coach.

'I think we have sorted it out now because I was talking to her the other day and I think the problem is that she struggles to talk to teenagers, as well as younger children. So that's where she struggles, but she can be nice.'

Laura now had an idea for a way for her and her friends to make things work: she was going to 'teach' the coach.

'Quite a few of us have moved into her group now, so she is going to have to learn.'

SELF-DETERMINATION

KEY TAKEAWAYS

The talent development environment is focused on the level of the athlete's ability and the judgement of potential. Motivating an athlete to pursue a performance pathway in his or her sport often depends on the motivational conditions created by the coach. It relies on the coach's ability to create an environment that satisfies three key psychological needs:

> 1) Autonomy
>
> As young athletes progress, they place more value on taking ownership of their development.
>
> 2) Connectedness
>
> Young people's identities, knowledge, capacities and skills are shaped in the relationships they build.
>
> 3) Competence
>
> An athlete's perception of his or her ability and self-belief is critical to proactive learning.

The true power of the talent development process lies in its ability to mobilise the athlete and coach to work towards achieving mutually agreed goals. When the young athlete becomes engaged with the coaching process (rather than subject to it), this leads to an increased sense of independence and empowerment. Empowerment enables young athletes to make informed decisions and choices to help take charge of their lives.

Independence and empowerment are supported when young athletes gain the maturity and experience necessary to better think through the consequences of their actions. Guidance from both coaches and parents are fundamental to this process. When young athletes receive advice that leads to (and supports) their improvement, they will tend to feel more competent and become more committed to their sport.

Young athletes seek equal relationships where power is shared and they are able to make informed decisions to take charge of their own development. These equal relationships often require the coaches and parents involved to concede their positions of power. This involves learning to both listen to and respect the opinions of their young athletes.

When this is done, it promotes the wellbeing of the athlete. By listening to their athletes, adults in talent development environments can demonstrate that they take their opinions seriously. The young athletes can also influence the thinking of their coaches and parents, potentially leading to better outcomes for everyone involved in each relationship.

TALENT DEVELOPMENT TIPS

◆ Autonomy, connectedness and a sense of competence are critical to the young athlete's motivation.

A different coach may facilitate a different experience for an athlete. The athlete should engage with and commit to the coach who adopts the approach that works best for his or her age and stage of development.

◆ Provide each athlete with positive options.

If the athlete does not feel able to make progress, work collaboratively to create an environment that suits his or her wants and needs, or support the athlete's transition to an alternative pathway.

◆ Each athlete will decide how long he or she continues on the performance pathway.

Encourage young athletes to trust themselves and to determine their own paths.

CHAPTER 6

SELF-REGULATION

In this chapter, you will gain insights into:

- ◆ How to teach the young athlete to become the best learner.
- ◆ Why you should model self-regulation.
- ◆ Why it is important to teach young people that setbacks and mistakes are part of learning.

JOSH'S STORY

FISHING IN THE DARK

Josh has been fishing since he was eight and he is on the talent pathway for the national angling team. He enjoys playing other sports and is a good all-round sportsman, but fishing is where he comes into his own.

WAITING

Josh was waiting. Waiting for the letter that would tell him if all his hard work had paid off. The letter that would confirm if he had made it through, if he had made the cut. If he did, there would be just one more trial and the prize at the end was the chance to fish for his country at the Junior World Championships in Holland.

The letter finally arrived. Before he opened it, Josh thought about what had gone before and what could lie ahead. He was anxious.

The trials were a big deal. He remembered the time when he received a letter for them on a Friday and it only gave him eight days to prepare. He had immediately rung his Grandad and said:

'I've got the letter, but we've only got a week.'

He had prepared his kit the same night and the next day he was there. Five hours on the bank with Grandad sitting behind him watching from the car. The experience lived vividly in his memory.

'Terrible conditions, blowing an absolute gale, wind, rain, freezing cold. So not really what you wanted, but I guess it was a good way to understand what the place was like.'

On the day of that trial, Josh couldn't believe it when he arrived and the organisers told him they had changed the lake! It threw him. His letter had clearly stated the lake where they would be fishing, and now they were telling him they hadn't been able to book it.

Some of the other anglers hadn't been for a practice

at the lake like Josh had, so they weren't affected. He had travelled down there twice to practise.

'What was the point?' he asked himself.

The trials were supposed to be for the national team, but they felt like a shambles. He had to go in *'blind'*. It was a real challenge but he persevered, felt his way into them, taught himself as he went along, learnt the new lake and came through.

This year it was a different challenge. The lake was the same but the fishing was different. It was the lake where he had practised but on the day of the trial he drew a peg that only gave him three metres of water to fish in. He was supposed to have eight metres. There was eight metres when he practised, and everyone else had eight!

Josh had to quickly change all his rigs and he started to panic. He knew that was the worst thing he could do. He told himself that he needed to *'keep his head on'*. He got himself together. Then, first drop in he got a fish, and his nerves started to settle. He knew he just had to keep repeating the process.

'It's making your body efficient enough to do it quickly, but not rushing, which is another skill, it's just patience and composure.'

He caught 150 fish. It was a good day, he knew he'd worked hard and done his best. There was nothing else he could do, but was it enough?

Josh opened the letter: he had made it through to the final trial!

But he knew there was no time to celebrate. His

thoughts immediately turned to the next test and he wanted to get to work.

'Now I've got to prepare for this one. I've got just over a month to prepare, so that will give me a lot more time to get down to the venue and understand it, which is a bit more important for this one. It's a bigger trial, there's going to be a lot more people there.'

Josh reflected on the letter. He was through but it gave him no feedback.

He wanted to know what he had done well.

Was there anything that he could do better?

What was it they were looking for?

But the coaches were funny like that. They didn't really tell you anything, it was just like a guessing game.

THE FINAL TRIAL

Josh knew that the national selectors were watching but he didn't know what they were looking for.

'You just don't know. You've just got to turn up, do what you do and see if they like you. They gotta like you. It's like any sport, if you haven't got the right attitude, they won't pick you. You gotta have a hard-working team.'

He did know that there were only three places available and so five anglers trialling wouldn't make it. The stakes were high and Josh was nervous.

'The thing with fishing is, you need your

hands .... you can't have them shaking. So I had to sit in the car for five minutes and just calm myself down, which is quite annoying but I know how to deal with it. So it's not too bad. But, yeah it was big, it was a big deal for me.'

Josh went to work. He worked with both his mind and his hands. The rod was like an extension of his arm. His action was a skill he had worked hard to develop and he relied on his consistent accuracy. He knew if he could cast to the same spot over and over again and keep the fish in the same area, then he could work them into a frenzy.

Josh needed to focus but all of a sudden he was distracted. He could feel eyes on his back. The national coach was sitting right behind him. *'That's a good thing,'* he told himself. *'If he keeps watching me, he must be interested?'*

But it started to make him edgy and that was a bad thing. He had to stop himself from shaking. The coach sat but he didn't say a word. They never do, they just watch.

Josh tried to concentrate. He wasn't sure if he was doing the right thing, it felt like a mind game. Nobody said anything.

Five hours passed. It was time for the weigh in. He had been in a poor area and knew he couldn't win the match, but he had aimed for the next best thing: to win his section.

'That's my mentality. If I do something, I want to win.'

He watched as each catch was weighed. It was a painful process. Had he done enough? The coaches always say that weight doesn't mean much. 'It doesn't matter what you catch,' but he knew it did. They want people catching fish consistently.

'At the end of the day, to win, you need to catch fish.'

THE BIG SHOCK

Josh was very upset and annoyed. He didn't know why he hadn't been selected. It had been a really long process. He had put in hours of hard work practising and travelling. He had won his section at the final trial and performed well.

'The only thing I can do is win my match .... 'Try your best,' they said and that's what I did, but apparently my best wasn't good enough.'

'It was such a harsh cut. Literally that's it, done, see you next year......... A big shock.'

It was over just like that. He was *'binned'*. To get so close and then to miss out was the most gutting thing. All he received was a letter telling him he hadn't been selected. Not even a phone call, no feedback, no areas to work on, nothing. Just a letter basically saying, 'Sorry you haven't got through, hope to see you next year'.

It was a nightmare. Josh was back to square one. The only way back in was to start again and work his way back. It really annoyed him. It really, really got to him.

How was he supposed to improve as an angler when he didn't know what he needed to improve? There are so many aspects to it. What had he done wrong? Josh had beaten his mate, but his mate was selected. He couldn't understand it. He thought it was both poor and frustrating at the same time.

> 'Talent development programs need to look at kids who don't get through and tell them what they need to know. When you get binned you don't know what to do, you question yourself.......... What did I do? What was wrong? What do I need to do now?...............You just have to work it out by yourself.'

Josh made a decision. He wasn't going to put himself through it all again next year. There was no point. He had put hours and hours into practising and improving, only to later learn that some of the anglers already knew they were in the team before the final trial. The selectors had made up their minds before they had even started fishing!

He knew he could get better and he wanted to improve, but he didn't see how the trials were going to help him do that. He was only 16 and had two more years to make the team. Josh decided he would take a year out, improve, hone his skills and then go for selection again. With more time, practice and experience, he still believed he could make the team.

Four weeks passed. Then another letter came. It was an invitation to travel with the National U18 team to the Junior World Championships in Holland!

The team would leave in a week. The selectors thought it would be good for him to experience the World Championships. He would not compete but he would get to fish. Josh was chuffed to bits. He jumped at the chance.

The World Championships opened his eyes. He learnt that the boys who had been selected were not like him. They didn't play rugby and cricket. All they did was fish.

Maybe he needed to be more like them?

Maybe he had a big decision to make?

While he was in Holland, the coaches asked Josh if he was going to go to the next set of trials. He told them he wasn't. He wanted to concentrate on his development and then trial again the following year. Josh didn't enjoy the trials and he didn't think he learnt anything from them. He didn't tell them that though!

The coaches told him they respected his decision and that he had made a wise choice. With another year practising and perfecting his techniques, he would be better prepared. He would be ready. In the meantime he could decide if he was prepared to give up his other sports. Whatever he decided, it would be up to him. There would be no more fishing in the dark for Josh.

SELF-REGULATION

KEY TAKEAWAYS

Self-regulation in the talent development context is the degree to which the athletes are proactive participants in their own learning. Athletes involved in sport at higher levels have learnt to be more goal-directed and more self-conscious. Higher-level athletes learn to self-regulate by exerting greater control over their feelings, thoughts and actions.

To be successful, young athletes must learn to be

self-aware, problem-focused and goal-oriented. They need to be proactive, independent, resourceful, and persistent. They also need to demonstrate initiative and to take responsibility for their actions.

Self-regulatory skills in athletes can be developed through feedback and instruction from coaches and parents. Young athletes who successfully self-regulate can recognise how an adult may help or hinder their learning.

Effective self-regulation depends on the athlete's selective use of specific skills. These skills include:

- setting specific goals
- adopting powerful strategies to achieve goals
- monitoring performance for signs of progress
- restructuring their physical and social environments to make them compatible with goals
- managing time efficiently
- accurate self-evaluation
- the ability to adapt to changing circumstances
- prioritising long term development over early success.

Successful athletes have superior self-regulatory skills. The level of learning achieved by athletes in sport varies depending on the presence or absence of these skills. Adults within the talent development context should aim to empower (not just support) their athletes via the development of their self-regulatory skills.

TALENT DEVELOPMENT TIPS

- Teach the young athlete to become the best learner.

    Parents and coaches need to create an environment that promotes self-regulation and independent learning.

- Model self-regulation.

    Coaches and parents should practise listening to learn versus listening to speak. They should share both what and how they are learning from young athletes.

- Teach young people that setbacks and mistakes are part of learning.

    Challenge young athletes to target things that are hard for them to do. Then guide and work with them to solve their problems and reach their goals.

CONCLUSION

Ultimately a talented athlete must become an expert learner to progress along the performance pathway. Expert learners possess high levels of self-belief in their ability to learn, perform successfully and control outcomes. Knowledge and understanding of how young athletes make sense of stages within the developmental process is critical to creating optimal environments to support talent development and transition.

The stories in this book demonstrate that the true power of talent development programs lies with their potential to connect with young athletes' desires, beliefs and attitudes. Conversation that engages young athletes as equal partners in an attempt to see the world from their perspective is the greatest tool for their empowerment.

The process of athlete empowerment therefore relies upon effective communication, collaboration and the sharing of power. It is essential that these conditions are created within the talent development experience. If young athletes feel as though they are being listened to and are active in decision-making about their learning and their lives, then they will feel better respected and understood. All adults in the talent development context need to find ways to make better connections with their young athletes. They need to provide each athlete with a voice that is heard.

Ultimately, the talent development experience of young athletes in sport is determined by the way they feel they have been treated by the adults involved in the process.

The following recommendations serve as a guide for interacting with young athletes:

- Promote trust and effective communication by getting to know them well.
- Provide opportunities for them to express and debate issues that are affecting their lives.
- Listen and respond to their views on matters that affect their sporting participation, selection and performance.
- Find ways to enable them to influence their practice and individualise their learning to ensure their health and wellbeing.

ACKNOWLEDGEMENTS

Thank you to my family, Fiona, Ria, Elliot and Romy for your love, wisdom and support.

Thank you to the young athletes who shared their stories.

Graham Turner

ABOUT THE AUTHOR

GRAHAM TURNER PHD, MSC, B.ED. (HONS), FHEA, ASCC

Graham has spent his career supporting and developing talented athletes and coaches across the world. His insights come from being a parent, coach, researcher and performance pathway systems leader. He has a PhD in Talent Development in Sport.

Graham began his career as a physical education teacher and football (soccer) coach. He has been Head of Physical Education and Sport at two schools in England and worked in youth development in professional football for Wolverhampton Wanderers, Nottingham Forest, Aston Villa, Crewe Alexandra, Bradford City and Leeds United.

He has also worked as a Senior Lecturer in Sports Coaching at Leeds Beckett University where he consulted on leading talent development practices for male and female athletes in a range of professional, Olympic and Commonwealth Games sports.

In Australia, Graham has worked as Coach and Athlete Development Consultant at the Northern Territory Institute of Sport, National Elite Coaching Manager for Gymnastics Australia, and he is currently a Performance Pathway Coach and Athlete Development Consultant at the Australian Institute of Sport.

References: Turner, G. (2016) Talent' mentalities: young people's experience of being in a sports talent development programme

If you would like to learn more about athlete development please connect to Graham by scanning the QR code below,

www.ingramcontent.com/pod-product-compliance
Lightning Source LLC
Chambersburg PA
CBHW051540010526
44107CB00064B/2792